This student workbook is intended to reinforce your understanding of the three units of substantive content (scientific explanations and evidence), plus the procedural content (How Science Works), on the new single award GCSE Chemistry specification from AQA.

Every worksheet is cross-referenced to the revision and classroom companion, *AQA GCSE Chemistry*, published by Letts and Lonsdale.

The questions in your objective tests / written exams will combine elements from both types of content, so to answer them you will have to recall relevant scientific facts and draw upon your knowledge of how science works.

The questions on pages 4–11 of this workbook will test your understanding of the key concepts covered in How Science Works. In addition, there are individual How Science Works question pages throughout this book, which are designed to make sure you know how to apply your knowledge, for example, to evaluate topical social-scientific issues.

HT In this workbook, any questions that cover content which will only be tested on Higher Tier test papers appear inside clearly labelled boxes.

A Note to Teachers

The pages in this workbook can be used as…

- classwork sheets – students can use the revision guide to answer the questions
- harder classwork sheets – pupils study the topic and then answer the questions without using the revision guide
- easy-to-mark homework sheets – to test pupils' understanding and reinforce their learning
- the basis for learning homework tasks which are then tested in subsequent lessons
- test material for topics or entire units
- a structured revision programme prior to the objective tests / written exams.

Answers to these worksheets are available to order.

ISBN: 978-1-905

03/090409

Published by Letts and Lonsdale

Project Editor: Tracey Cowell
Cover and Concept Design: Sarah Duxbury
Design: Little Red Dog Design

Letts and Lonsdale make every effort to ensure that all paper used in our books is made from wood pulp obtained from well-managed forests, controlled sources and recycled wood or fibre.

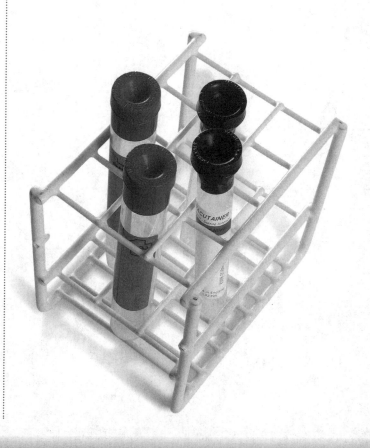

Contents

Contents

The numbers in brackets correspond to the reference numbers on the AQA GCSE Chemistry specification.

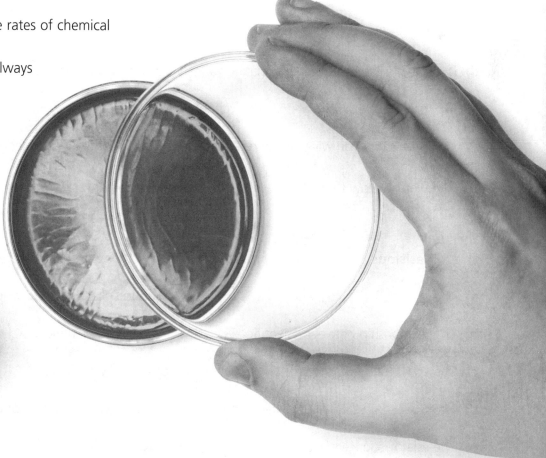

How Science Works

How Science Works

The following questions are designed to make sure you understand what the How Science Works element of your AQA GCSE science course is all about.

1 Only one statement in each of the following sets is accurate. Read them all carefully and then place a tick beside the correct one.

a) **i)** The term 'How Science Works' refers to a set of key concepts. ☐

ii) The term 'How Science Works' refers to a set of unanswered questions. ☐

iii) The term 'How Science Works' refers to a set of scientific facts. ☐

b) **i)** How Science Works is only relevant to chemistry. ☐

ii) How Science Works is relevant to all areas of science. ☐

iii) How Science Works only refers to past scientific work. ☐

c) **i)** How Science Works is normally taught separately. ☐

ii) How Science Works is normally taught alongside the science content. ☐

iii) How Science Works is not taught in the classroom. ☐

d) **i)** There will be no questions relating to How Science Works in the exam. ☐

ii) There will be a separate exam covering How Science Works. ☐

iii) In the exam you will need to recall facts and draw upon your knowledge of How Science Works. ☐

2 Use the words below to fill the spaces and complete the sentences, which outline the main areas covered by How Science Works.

society   practices   reliability   explanations
     decisions   procedures   evidence   validity

a) The .... and .... used to collect scientific evidence.

b) The relationship between scientific .... and scientific .... and theories.

c) The .... and .... of scientific evidence.

d) How .... are made about the use of science and technology.

e) The role of science in ....

What is the Purpose of Science?

1 Below are ten statements about science. Read them carefully and then place a tick alongside the ones that are correct.

a) Scientific understanding can lead to the development of new technologies. ☐

b) Science looks for solutions to problems. ☐

c) Science is unconcerned with facts and evidence. ☐

d) Science tries to determine how and why things happen. ☐

e) Scientific knowledge has little relevance in the modern world. ☐

f) Scientific breakthroughs can have a huge impact on society. ☐

g) Scientific knowledge is only useful if you work in medicine. ☐

h) Science attempts to explain the world we live in. ☐

i) Scientific discoveries can have an impact on the environment. ☐

j) Science does not affect our everyday lives. ☐

Scientific Evidence

2 In your own words, describe the purpose of scientific evidence.

....

....

....

3 Scientific evidence is often based on data. Name two methods of collecting data.

a) ....

b) ....

4 It is important for scientific evidence to be reliable and valid.

a) What is meant by the term **reliable**? ....

b) What is meant by the term **valid**? ....

c) *Data can be valid, even if it is not reliable.* Is this statement **true** or **false**? ....

d) Why does data need to be reliable and valid?

How Science Works

Observations

1 The following phrases all refer to important stages in scientific research. Number them **1** to **6**, to show the order in which they normally take place.

a) Analyse the data ☐

b) Develop a hypothesis ☐

c) Make an observation ☐

d) Amend the hypothesis ☐

e) Carry out an investigation ☐

f) Make a prediction ☐

2 a) Write **true** or **false**, as appropriate, alongside each of these statements about hypotheses.

i) A hypothesis summarises a number of related observations. ....

ii) A hypothesis is a statement which suggests an explanation for something. ....

iii) A hypothesis is a question which asks why a phenomenon occurs. ....

iv) A hypothesis normally proposes a relationship between two variables. ....

v) A hypothesis is a conclusion based on scientific data. ....

b) What are hypotheses based on?

....

3 What must happen if new observations, and related data, do not match existing theories and explanations relating to the same phenomenon?

....

Investigations

1 What is the purpose of a scientific investigation?

_____

_____

2 In a scientific investigation there are two variables: the independent variable and the dependent variable. In the space below, write a short definition for each to help you remember the difference.

a) Independent variable

_____

_____

b) Dependent variable

_____

_____

3 A student predicts that water will evaporate at a faster rate if room temperature is increased.

For his investigation he places a beaker containing water in three different rooms. Each room is kept at a different temperature: 15°C, 20°C and 25°C.

He measures the amount of water remaining in each beaker every 24 hours.

a) Which is the independent variable in this investigation? Explain your answer.

_____

_____

b) Which is the dependent variable in this investigation? Explain your answer.

_____

_____

c) Is the dependent variable **continuous**, **discrete**, **ordered** or **categoric**? _____

d) Identify one other variable that could affect the results of this investigation.

_____

How Science Works

Investigations (cont.)

4 For each example below, state whether the link between the two variables, x and y, is **causal**, **due to association**, or **due to chance**.

a) Variables x and y appear to be related, because an increase in x coincides with an increase in y. However, a scientific investigation finds that they are both acting independently.

_____

b) Variables x and y both start to decrease at the same time. A scientific investigation finds that the decreases in x and y are both the result of an increase in variable z.

_____

c) A scientific investigation finds that a change in variable x brings about a change in variable y.

_____

5 a) What is a fair test?

_____

_____

b) In general terms, how can you ensure a fair test?

_____

_____

c) Why is it often easier to achieve a fair test in laboratory conditions than in the field (e.g. when carrying out an investigation into the effects of pollutants on the environment)?

_____

_____

6 When conducting a scientific survey, why is it important to ensure that the individuals in the sample are closely matched?

_____

_____

_____

Investigations (cont.)

7 The following passage describes how a control experiment can be used in a scientific investigation. The words **dependent**, **independent** and **data** have been deleted. Insert them into the correct spaces to complete the passage.

Scientists collect .... by carrying out investigations. For example, they might set up an

experiment in which they can make controlled changes to the .... variable and then

measure the .... variable.

In a control experiment, the .... variable is not changed, but the ....

variable is still measured. This provides a second set of ....

By comparing the two sets of ...., the investigator can establish whether changes to

the .... variable were caused by the .... variable.

If the .... variable shows the same changes in the control experiment, then they

cannot have been caused by the .... variable.

8 a) In an investigation, why is it a good idea to repeat the measurements and then calculate their mean?

....

....

b) What is the standard formula for calculating the mean of a set of measurements?

....

c) Calculate the mean of the following set of data (show your working).

Measurement	Temperature (°C)
1	45.2
2	44.8
3	44.7
4	45.0
5	44.7

Answer: ....

How Science Works

Measurements

1 Name three factors that can affect the reliability and validity of measurements.

a) ....

b) ....

c) ....

2 A student repeats the same measurement ten times. She notices that one of the readings is very different from the rest of the data. In your own words, explain what she should do next.

....

....

....

Presenting Data

3 Suggest two benefits of presenting data in an appropriate graph or chart.

a) ....

b) ....

4 A meteorologist measures the air temperature in degrees Celsius (°C) every 60 minutes. What type of graph could best be used to display this data? Explain your answer.

....

....

....

Conclusions

5 Write **true** or **false**, as appropriate, alongside each of the following statements about scientific conclusions.

Conclusions should…

a) include speculation and personal opinion. ....

b) describe the patterns and relationships shown in the data. ....

c) take all the data into account. ....

d) only refer to the bits of data that support the hypothesis. ....

e) make direct reference to the original hypothesis. ....

Conclusions (cont.)

5 List three points that need to be considered in an evaluation.

a) ....

b) ....

c) ....

6 Suggest one way in which the reliability of an investigation can be improved.

....

7 Use a line to connect each type of issue with the area it is concerned with.

Social issues	Money and resources
Economic issues	Morals and value judgements
Environmental issues	The human population
Ethical issues	The Earth's ecosystems

8 a) List the three things you should always consider when asked to evaluate information about social-scientific issues.

i) P................................ ii) M................................ iii) I................................

b) Name three factors that could influence the reliability of information about social-scientific issues.

i) .... ii) .... iii) ....

9 *Science can answer all questions.*

Is this statement **true** or **false**? Explain your answer.

....

....

....

Atoms

1 Label the two main parts of an atom on the diagram below.

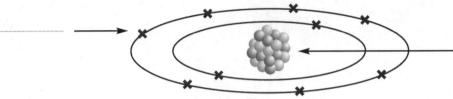

Elements

2 a) What do we mean by the term **element**, and how many elements are there?

_____

_____

b) Where and how are elements grouped together?

_____

_____

c) Give the chemical symbols for the following elements:

Oxygen _____

Carbon _____

Iron _____

Compounds

3 a) What is a compound?

_____

_____

_____

b) When elements react, how can the atoms form chemical bonds?

_____

_____

Chemical Formulae

1 a) In terms of elements and atoms, what do chemical formulae show?

....

....

b) Insert brackets and mathematical functions to show what the following chemical formulae mean. The first one has been done for you.

KNO$_3$ = (1 x K) + (1 x N) + (3 x O)

i) 2NaCl ....

ii) 3Al$_2$O$_3$ ....

iii) Ca(OH)$_2$ ....

c) In the spaces provided write down the number of molecules and the number of atoms in each of the compounds shown below. The first one has been done for you.

Chemical Formula	Number of Molecules	Number of Atoms
2H$_2$O	2	2(2 x H) = 4 x H 2(1 x O) = 2 x O
3ZnO		
NaOH		
4H$_2$SO$_4$		

Chemical Reactions

2 a) When you write a word equation, what are the reactants and products?

i) Reactants: ....

ii) Products: ....

b) Label the reactants and the products in the following equation:

Magnesium + Oxygen ⟶ Magnesium oxide

....

Writing Balanced Equations

1 Explain what is meant when a chemical equation is said to be **balanced**.

_____

_____

2 a) Write down the word equation for the reaction shown in the table below.

Reactants			⟶	Products
....	+	....	⟶	....
Cu	+	O_2	⟶	CuO

b) Use the diagram below to explain how you would balance the equation.

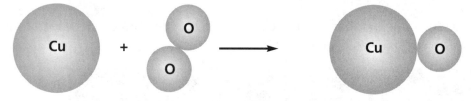

c) Write down the balanced symbol equation for this chemical reaction.

_____

Limestone

1 a) What is the main compound in limestone?

_____

b) Give three reasons why natural limestone is exploited?

i) _____ **ii)** _____ **iii)** _____

2 Some soil types are quite acidic. Slaked lime can be used to neutralise these soils.

a) What does the term **neutralise** mean?

_____

b) Complete the two word equations below to show how slaked lime (calcium hydroxide) is made from calcium carbonate.

i) Calcium carbonate	Heat →	_____ + _____ (quicklime)
ii) _____	+ Water →	Calcium hydroxide (slaked lime)

c) Explain the advantages of using slaked lime instead of powdered limestone to neutralise acidic soil.

_____

3 a) Limestone is used to make glass. Describe the process.

_____

_____

_____

b) Briefly describe the process of producing cement.

_____

_____

c) Concrete is produced from cement. Name the three other materials which are also needed to make cement.

i) _____ **ii)** _____ **iii)** _____

How Science Works

To answer the questions on this page, you will have to recall scientific facts and draw upon your knowledge of how science works, e.g. scientific procedures, issues and ideas.

1 Complete the table below to show the four main uses of limestone and how it is extracted.

Use	Process of Extraction
	Quarried and cut into blocks.
Neutralising agent	
	Mix limestone, sand and soda, and heat until it melts. When cool, it is transparent.
Making cement, mortar and concrete	

2 Exploiting limestone has an impact on the environment, society and the economy.

a) List two advantages of quarrying limestone to produce building materials.

i) .... ii) ....

b) List two disadvantages of quarrying limestone to produce building materials.

i) .... ii) ....

c) Think in more detail about one of the disadvantages you have given. Consider the effects and consequences and discuss them briefly below.

....

....

....

....

How Science Works

To answer the questions on this page, you will have to recall scientific facts and draw upon your knowledge of how science works, e.g. scientific procedures, issues and ideas.

3 a) List one advantage and one disadvantage of using limestone, concrete and glass as building materials.

Material	Advantage	Disadvantage
i) Limestone		
ii) Concrete		
iii) Glass		

b) Why are these materials often a better choice for construction than wood?

c) Consider other potential building materials. Use the Internet, school library or another secondary resource to research one alternative and discuss reasons why it might be suitable to use.

Unit 1 – 11.2

Ores

1 Describe briefly what an ore is.

Extracting Metals from their Ores

2 a) The method used for extracting a metal depends on how reactive it is.

    i) Name one unreactive metal and describe briefly how it is obtained.

    ii) Briefly describe how you extract a metal from its oxide.

    iii) What is this process called?

  b) How are metals that are less reactive than carbon extracted from their oxides?

Iron

3 a) What does molten iron contain?

  b) How can the properties of iron be changed?

  c) Name one common alloy produced from iron.

Alloys

1 a) What is an alloy?

_____

b) Explain why alloys are usually stronger and harder than the pure metals used to make them.

_____

_____

Steel

2 a) Briefly describe the process of making steel.

_____

_____

_____

_____

b) Complete the table below to show how the elements that are added to steel determine its properties.

Element(s) in Steel	Properties	Common Example
_____	Hard and strong	Screwdrivers
Low carbon content	_____	Cars
_____	Hard and resistant to corrosion	_____

Smart Alloys

3 Smart alloys are being developed to meet the demands of modern engineering and manufacturing. Name one product made from a smart alloy and briefly describe how the material is suited to its purpose.

_____

_____

_____

The Transition Metals

1 a) List three transition metals.

i) ....

ii) ....

iii) ....

b) Give three reasons why transition metals are useful as structural materials, and as electrical and thermal conductors.

i) ....

ii) ....

iii) ....

Extracting Transition Metals

2 a) Name the process used to extract copper, aluminium and titanium. ....

b) List three reasons why recycling metals is important.

i) ....

ii) ....

iii) ....

Copper, Aluminium and Titanium

3 Complete the table below to show the properties and uses of copper, aluminium and titanium.

Transition Metal	Properties	Uses
....	Limited natural supplies	....
Titanium	....	Aeroplanes Replacement hip joints
....	Low density / light	Window frames

To answer the questions on this page, you will have to recall scientific facts and draw upon your knowledge of how science works, e.g. scientific procedures, issues and ideas.

1 Complete the table below to remind yourself how different metals are obtained.

Metal	How it is Obtained
	Physical extraction, e.g. panning
Metal oxides	
Iron	
	Molten iron from a blast furnace is transferred to another furnace. It is mixed with recycled scrap metal, and pure oxygen is passed into the mixture. The oxygen reacts with non-metal impurities such as carbon, silicon and sulfur to produce acidic oxides.
Copper, aluminium and titanium	

2 Exploiting metals has an impact on the environment, society and the economy. Give one advantage and one disadvantage of a) extracting and b) recycling metals.

a) Advantage of extraction   Disadvantage of extraction

   i) ....   **ii)** ....

b) Advantage of recycling   Disadvantage of recycling

   i) ....   **ii)** ....

How Science Works

To answer the questions on this page, you will have to recall scientific facts and draw upon your knowledge of how science works, e.g. scientific procedures, issues and ideas.

1 **a)** Describe briefly why alloys, rather than pure metals, are better suited for everyday use.

....

b) List three products made from steel.

   i) ....

   ii) ....

   iii) ....

c) List three products made from smart alloys.

   i) ....

   ii) ....

   iii) ....

2 Think about the advantages and disadvantages of using metals as structural materials and as smart materials.

With this in mind, choose one of the products you listed above. Consider why steel or smart alloys, as opposed to other metals or materials, are used to make the product. Discuss below.

....

....

....

....

....

....

....

....

....

Crude Oil

1 Crude oil is a mixture of hydrocarbons.

a) What does the term **mixture** mean?

....

....

b) What is a **hydrocarbon**?

....

c) Name the process by which crude oil can be separated.

....

d) The table below shows the boiling point of five hydrocarbons. Use the information to answer the following questions.

Hydrocarbon	Boiling Point (°C)
A	180
B	90
C	120
D	45
E	135

i) Which hydrocarbon flows most easily? ....

ii) Which hydrocarbon is the least flammable? ....

iii) Which hydrocarbon is the least volatile? ....

e) Put the hydrocarbons, A to E, in order of the number of hydrogen and carbon atoms contained in one molecule.

Least number of hydrogen and carbon atoms ⟶ Greatest number of hydrogen and carbon atoms

....	....	....	....	....

Fractional Distillation

2 Describe the process by which the different fractions of crude oil are separated in a fractionating column.

....

....

Alkanes

1 Decane is an alkane that has the formula $C_{10}H_{22}$.

a) Explain the meaning of the word **alkane**.

....

....

b) Draw the displayed formula for decane.

c) When decane is heated in the presence of a catalyst the following reaction takes place:

$$C_{10}H_{22} \longrightarrow C_XH_Y + C_2H_4$$

Use the equation to work out the formula for C_XH_Y.

....

....

2 a) Why are alkanes fairly unreactive compounds?

....

....

....

b) Why are shorter-chain hydrocarbons in greater demand as fuels?

....

....

....

How Science Works

To answer the questions on this page, you will have to recall scientific facts and draw upon your knowledge of how science works, e.g. scientific procedures, issues and ideas.

1 a) Give one advantage or disadvantage of using fossil fuels that has an effect on the human population, i.e. a social impact.

_____

b) Give one advantage or disadvantage of using fossil fuels that is concerned with money, i.e. an economic impact.

_____

c) Give one advantage or disadvantage of using fossil fuels that has an effect on the environment, i.e. an environmental impact.

_____

2 Ethanol and hydrogen are two potential alternative energy sources.

a) List one advantage and one disadvantage of using each of these fuels.

Fuel	Advantage	Disadvantage
i) Ethanol		
ii) Hydrogen		

b) Find out more about the production of hydrogen (e.g. through the Internet, school library or another secondary source). Do you think it would make a viable alternative to fossil fuels? Explain your answer.

_____

_____

_____

_____

_____

Cracking Hydrocarbons

1 a) What do we mean by **cracking** long-chain hydrocarbons? Draw a diagram to help illustrate your answer.

....

....

....

b) During cracking, the hydrocarbons are passed over a broken pot catalyst. What does this catalyst do?

....

c) Name two of the products of cracking.

i) ....   **ii)** ....

Making Alcohol from Ethene

2 a) Ethanol is a member of the alcohol family. How is it produced?

....

....

b) List three uses of ethanol.

i) ....   **ii)** ....

iii) ....

Alkenes (Unsaturated Hydrocarbons)

3 a) What is an **alkene**?

....

b) Complete the table below.

Name of Hydrocarbon	Propane	
Formula		C_3H_6
Structural Formula		

Polymerisation

1 a) Why are alkenes very reactive?

....

b) Briefly describe the process of polymerisation.

....

....

....

....

Making Poly(ethene) from Ethene

2 Many molecules of ethene can be joined together to form poly(ethene). What needs to happen to each ethene molecule in order for this to happen?

....

....

Representing Addition Polymerisation

3 Complete the following equation to show how three ethene molecules join together to form part of a poly(ethene) molecule.

$$\underset{H}{\overset{H}{\diagdown}}C=C\underset{H}{\overset{H}{\diagup}} \quad + \quad \underset{H}{\overset{H}{\diagdown}}C=C\underset{H}{\overset{H}{\diagup}} \quad + \quad \underset{H}{\overset{H}{\diagdown}}C=C\underset{H}{\overset{H}{\diagup}} \quad \longrightarrow$$

General Formula for Addition Polymerisation

4 a) Draw the structural formula for a poly(ethene) molecule containing 'n' ethene molecules.

b) What is the name of the polymer formed from chloroethene?

....

Polymers

1 Polymers have many uses and new uses are being developed.

a) List three current uses of polymers.

i) ....

ii) ....

iii) ....

b) Complete the following table showing the different uses of specific polymers.

Polymer	Uses
....	Waterproof items Electrical insulation Drain pipes
Polystyrene	....
....	Plastic bags Bottles
Poly(propene)	....

2 List two methods of plastic disposal that can have an impact on the environment. Provide one reason why each of these methods can have a harmful effect.

a) ....

....

b) ....

....

How Science Works

To answer the questions on this page, you will have to recall scientific facts and draw upon your knowledge of how science works, e.g. scientific procedures, issues and ideas.

1 a) List two social and / or economic advantages and disadvantages of using products made from crude oil.

Advantages

i) ....

ii) ....

Disadvantages

iii) ....

iv) ....

b) Imagine that the use of crude oil was banned. Describe four ways in which this would affect society and the economy in the UK. (Hint: think about employment and how the products of crude oil are used.)

....

....

....

....

....

....

....

2 a) Why are polymers so useful? List two advantages below.

i) ....

ii) ....

b) Consider the environmental effects of using, disposing of, and recycling polymers.
List three disadvantages of polymers.

i) ....

ii) ....

iii) ....

How Science Works

To answer the questions on this page, you will have to recall scientific facts and draw upon your knowledge of how science works, e.g. scientific procedures, issues and ideas.

1 a) Briefly describe how ethanol is produced from i) renewable and ii) non-renewable sources.

i) Using renewable sources

_____

_____

_____

_____

_____

ii) Using non-renewable sources

_____

_____

_____

b) List two advantages and one disadvantage of using renewable sources to produce ethanol.

Advantages

i) _____

ii) _____

Disadvantage

iii) _____

c) List two advantages and one disadvantage of using non-renewable sources to produce ethanol.

Advantages

i) _____

ii) _____

Disadvantage

iii) _____

Getting Oil from Plants

1 a) Name three oils that are extracted from plants and used in consumer products.

i) ....

ii) ....

iii) ....

b) What are the two processes by which oil can be extracted from plant material?

i) .... ii) ....

Vegetable Oils

2 a) Vegetable oils are **unsaturated**. What does the term **unsaturated** mean?

....

b) Complete the following statements:

i) Vegetable oils can be detected using b__ __ __ __ __ __ w__ __ __ __.

ii) A mixture of oil and water is called an   __ __ __ l__ __ __ __.

c) i) Draw the structural formula equation for the production of dibromoethene from ethene and bromine water.

....

ii) What happens to the bromine atoms during this reaction?

....

....

d) Why will oil not dissolve in water?

....

e) Briefly explain why a chef might add mustard to a dressing made from olive oil and vinegar.

....

Unit 1 – 11.5

The Manufacture of Margarine

1 In general, the more double carbon carbon bonds there are in a substance, the lower its melting point.

a) How can you raise the melting point of an oil to produce a solid fat?

b) What is the name of the process illustrated in the structural formula equation below?

$$\begin{array}{ccccc}
\text{H} & \text{H} & & \text{H} & \text{H} \\
| & | & & | & | \\
\text{C} = \text{C} + \text{H}_2 & \xrightarrow{\text{Catalyst}} & \text{H} - \text{C} - \text{C} - \text{H} \\
| & | & & | & | \\
\text{H} & \text{H} & & \text{H} & \text{H}
\end{array}$$

c) Write a general word equation for this type of reaction.

Additives

2 a) What is the purpose of using additives?

b) What is an E-number?

3 Briefly describe the process of chromatography.

To answer the questions on this page, you will have to recall scientific facts and draw upon your knowledge of how science works, e.g. scientific procedures, issues and ideas.

1 a) Why are fats and oils an important food group?

....

b) Name one health risk associated with eating too many saturated fats.

....

c) In terms of its molecular structure, what is a saturated fat?

....

d) Describe the health benefits associated with monounsaturated fats.

....

....

....

2 a) In terms of sustainable development, why would it be sensible to increase the production and use of fuels made from vegetable oil?

....

....

....

....

b) Name three advantages to using fuels produced from vegetable oil as transport fuels.

i) ....

ii) ....

iii) ....

c) Name three disadvantages to using fuels produced from vegetable oil as transport fuels.

i) ....

ii) ....

iii) ....

How Science Works

To answer the questions on this page, you will have to recall scientific facts and draw upon your knowledge of how science works, e.g. scientific procedures, issues and ideas.

3 **a)** Complete the table below to show the range of food additives and their uses.

Type of Additive	Example	Use
Colourings	Curcumin E100	
	Monosodium glutamate E621	Enhances and replaces flavours that can be lost during processing.
	Lecithin E322	Mixes ingredients that would normally separate, to give a consistent texture.
Antioxidants		Helps to stop substances combining with oxygen in the air, which would make the food 'go off'.
Preservatives	Sulfur dioxide E220	
	Sorbitol E420	Makes food taste sweeter.

b) List two advantages of using additives in foods.

i) ....

ii) ....

c) List two disadvantages of using additives in foods.

i) ....

ii) ....

d) Find out more about one of the additives included in the table above (e.g. using the Internet, school library or another secondary source). Discuss briefly the advantages and risks of using it in your food.

....

....

Structure of the Earth

1 a) Use the information below to draw a diagram showing the structure of the Earth. Draw the diagram to a scale of 1cm : 1000km and label it.

Layer	Inner Core	Outer Core	Mantle	Crust
Distance from Centre of Earth (km)	0 to 1500	1500 to 3300	3300 to 6300	6300 to 6400

b) Briefly describe the process known as the **rock cycle**.

Tectonic Theory

2 What two pieces of evidence relating to the east coast of South America and the west coast of Africa led scientists to believe that the features of the Earth's surface were not caused by shrinkage?

a)

b)

Tectonic Theory (cont.)

1 a) Summarise the main ideas behind Wegener's theory.

....

....

....

....

b) What phenomenon was Wegener unable to explain?

....

2 a) Fill in the missing words to complete the passage below, which describes how the tectonic plates move.

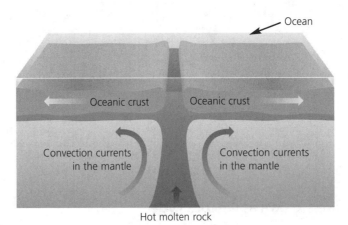

Convection .... in the Earth's .... push hot molten rock upwards.

At the plate .... , the molten rock rises to the surface. When the molten rock

.... down it forms new crust, pushing the .... plates slowly apart.

b) What natural hazards commonly occur at the boundaries where tectonic plates meet?

....

c) Why is it difficult for scientists to predict when these natural hazards will occur?

....

....

Tectonic Plate Movement

1 Using the theory of tectonic plate movement, explain why earthquakes occur along the Californian coast of America.

_____

_____

_____

_____

2 a) In your own words, explain what is meant by a **constructive** plate margin.

_____

_____

_____

b) In your own words, explain what is meant by a **destructive** plate margin.

_____

_____

_____

c) Two different plate margins are shown on the diagram below. Clearly label which is constructive and which is destructive.

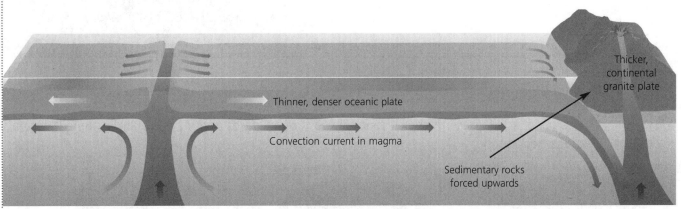

Thinner, denser oceanic plate

Convection current in magma

Thicker, continental granite plate

Sedimentary rocks forced upwards

Magma rising and solidifying to form new ocean floor (few centimetres per year)

Magma rising up through continental crust

The Earth's Atmosphere

1 The Earth was formed 4.6 billion years ago.

Complete the following table to show how the atmosphere has changed over this time.

	Composition of the Atmosphere	Reasons for Change
Formation of the Earth	Large proportion of carbon dioxide.	
3.5 billion years ago	Decrease in carbon dioxide, methane and ammonia. Increase in oxygen and nitrogen.	Green plants evolve. Carbon dioxide is reduced as the plants take it in and give out oxygen. Carbon from carbon dioxide in the air becomes locked up in sedimentary rocks as carbonates and fossil fuels. Methane and ammonia react with oxygen to release nitrogen (from the ammonia), which is also produced by bacteria removing nitrates from decaying plant material.
1.5 billion years ago		Some of the oxygen is converted into ozone which forms a thin layer in the atmosphere to filter out harmful UV light from the Sun. This reduction in harmful ultraviolet light allows the evolution of new living organisms, which increases oxygen and nitrogen further.
Present day		

2 Which of these pie charts represents the current composition of gases in the Earth's atmosphere? Place a tick beside the correct option.

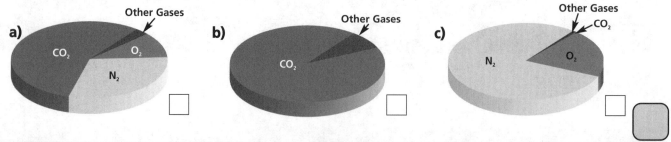

a)

b)

c)

Composition of the Atmosphere

1 a) List the main components that make up our atmosphere.

i) ....

ii) ....

iii) ....

iv) ....

b) Which two of these components have the highest percentages? Give the component and the percentage.

i) .... = ... %

ii) .... = ... %

c) Which component has the smallest percentage?

.... = ... %

d) Draw an accurate pie chart to show this information in the box alongside.

Changes to the Atmosphere

2 The level of carbon dioxide in the atmosphere is increasing.

Give two reasons why this is happening.

a) ....

b) ....

3 Higher levels of carbon dioxide in the atmosphere increase the rate of reaction that takes place between carbon dioxide and sea water.

a) What are the two products of this reaction?

i) ....

ii) ....

b) What do these products form?

....

How Science Works

To answer the questions on this page, you will have to recall scientific facts and draw upon your knowledge of how science works, e.g. scientific procedures, issues and ideas.

1 Until the early 1900s, nobody produced any evidence to contradict the theory of the Earth shrinking.

a) In 1915, who proposed the idea that led to the development of modern Tectonic Theory?

....

b) Briefly summarise the explanations that he proposed.

....

....

....

2 In the 1950s, scientists found new evidence to support the theory, and discovered that although some aspects of it were incorrect, the basis for the theory was well founded.

Briefly describe the Tectonic Theory that was developed as a result.

....

....

....

....

3 **a)** Briefly describe how earthquakes occur.

....

....

b) Why does this process mean that scientists cannot predict exactly when earthquakes will occur?

....

4 Scientists have sophisticated equipment to monitor volcano activity and areas prone to earthquakes.

Use the library, Internet or another secondary source to find out more about one piece of monitoring equipment. Briefly discuss why, despite having this instrument, scientists still cannot accurately predict when earthquakes and volcanic eruptions will occur.

....

....

....

How Science Works

To answer the questions on this page, you will have to recall scientific facts and draw upon your knowledge of how science works, e.g. scientific procedures, issues and ideas.

1 a) Complete the table below to explain the impact of human activities on our atmosphere

Human Activity	Pollutant	Impact on our Atmosphere
....	Sulfur dioxide Carbon dioxide	Sulfur dioxide contributes to the formation of acid rain, which can erode buildings and add acid to lakes and soils.
Increase in population and deforestation	Carbon dioxide	....
....	Carbon monoxide	Carbon monoxide eventually oxidises into carbon dioxide, increasing the amount of greenhouse gases, which leads to global warming.

b) Think in more detail about one of these human activities. Use the library, Internet or another secondary source to find out more about the impact this process has on our atmosphere. Summarise your findings below.

....

....

....

....

2 List three ways in which we can help to reduce the amount of pollutants in our atmosphere.

a) ....

b) ....

c) ....

1 Find the answers to the following clues in the wordsearch below. The definitions all relate to your learning in Unit 1.

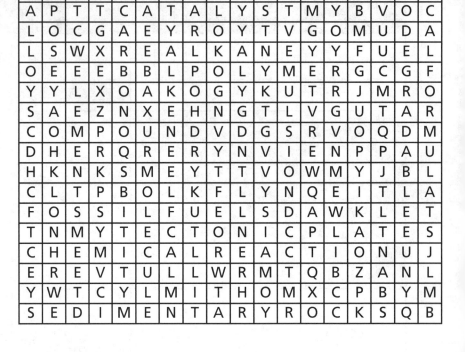

S	D	B	A	H	N	O	L	Q	T	S	Z	P	I	L	M	N	C
M	E	J	H	Y	D	R	O	G	E	N	A	T	I	O	N	O	H
A	C	S	B	D	G	H	N	S	B	Y	J	D	T	K	N	N	E
R	O	N	H	R	D	B	M	T	S	A	N	A	N	U	M	B	M
T	M	X	B	O	T	N	Y	R	S	X	U	I	T	B	E	I	I
A	P	T	T	C	A	T	A	L	Y	S	T	M	Y	B	V	O	C
L	O	C	G	A	E	Y	R	O	Y	T	V	G	O	M	U	D	A
L	S	W	X	R	E	A	L	K	A	N	E	Y	Y	F	U	E	L
O	E	E	E	B	B	L	P	O	L	Y	M	E	R	G	C	G	F
Y	Y	L	X	O	A	K	O	G	Y	K	U	T	R	J	M	R	O
S	A	E	Z	N	X	E	H	N	G	T	L	V	G	U	T	A	R
C	O	M	P	O	U	N	D	V	D	G	S	R	V	O	Q	D	M
D	H	E	R	Q	R	E	R	Y	N	V	I	E	N	P	P	A	U
H	K	N	K	S	M	E	Y	T	T	V	O	W	M	Y	J	B	L
C	L	T	P	B	O	L	K	F	L	Y	N	Q	E	I	T	L	A
F	O	S	S	I	L	F	U	E	L	S	D	A	W	K	L	E	T
T	N	M	Y	T	E	C	T	O	N	I	C	P	L	A	T	E	S
C	H	E	M	I	C	A	L	R	E	A	C	T	I	O	N	U	J
E	R	E	V	T	U	L	L	W	R	M	T	Q	B	Z	A	N	L
Y	W	T	C	Y	L	M	I	T	H	O	M	X	C	P	B	Y	M
S	E	D	I	M	E	N	T	A	R	Y	R	O	C	K	S	Q	B

a) 3 letters A natural mineral from which a metal can be extracted.

b) 4 letters **i)** The smallest part of an element which can enter into chemical reactions.

ii) A substance that releases heat or energy when combined with oxygen.

c) 5 letters A mixture of two or more metals or a mixture of one metal and a non-metal.

d) 6 letters **i)** A saturated hydrocarbon.

ii) An unsaturated hydrocarbon.

e) 7 letters **i)** A substance that consists of only one type of atom.

ii) A giant long-chained molecule.

f) 8 letters **i)** A substance that increases the rate of a reaction, whilst remaining chemically unchanged.

ii) A substance consisting of two or more elements combined together.

iii) A mixture of two liquids in which small globules of one of the liquids is suspended in the other.

iv) The simplest structural unit of an element or compound.

g) 9 letters To break down.

h) 10 letters An alloy which can change shape and then return to its original shape (2 words).

i) 11 letters **i)** Fuels formed over millions of years, from the remains of dead plants and animals.

ii) A compound containing only hydrogen and carbon.

j) 13 letters The process in which hydrogen is used to harden vegetable oils.

k) 14 letters Huge sections of the Earth's crust which move relative to one another (2 words).

l) 15 letters A representation of a substance using symbols for its constituent elements (2 words).

m) 16 letters **i)** A process in which one or more substances are changed into others (2 words).

ii) A substance that does not decompose naturally.

iii) Rocks formed by the accumulation of sediment in water or from air (2 words).

Subatomic Particles

1 a) Complete the table about atomic particles.

Atomic Particle	Relative Charge
....	+1
....	....
Electron	....

b) Describe the structure of an atom in terms of the particles in part **a)**.

....

....

....

2 a) Protons, neutrons and electrons have relative electrical charges. Explain briefly why atoms of a particular element have no overall charge.

....

....

b) Atoms of different elements have different numbers of protons. What is the number of protons in an atom otherwise known as?

....

c) i) What does an electron configuration tell us?

....

....

ii) The electron configuration of aluminium is 2,8,3. Briefly describe below what these numbers mean.

....

....

....

Unit 2 – 12.1 & 12.2

Electronic Structure

1 How are elements arranged in the periodic table?

The Alkali Metals (Group 1)

2 **a)** Why do all of the elements in Group 1 have similar properties?

b) What is produced when Group 1 elements react with non-metal elements?

The Halogens (Group 7)

3 **a)** Why do all of the elements in Group 7 have similar properties?

b) What is produced when Group 7 elements react with alkali metals?

Compounds and Mixtures

4 **a)** I consist of two or more elements or compounds that are not chemically combined together. The properties of the substances remain unchanged and specific to that substance. What am I?

b) We are substances in which the atoms of two or more elements are chemically combined (not just mixed together). What are we?

5 What are the two ways in which atoms can form chemical bonds?

a)

b)

Unit 2 – 12.1 & 12.2

The Ionic Bond

1 Calcium and chlorine react together to produce calcium chloride. The equation for this reaction is:

$$Ca + Cl_2 \longrightarrow CaCl_2$$

a) Use the Periodic Table at the back of this book to find the atomic numbers for…

i) calcium: _____   **ii)** chlorine: _____

b) Draw electron configuration diagrams for **i)** a calcium atom and **ii)** a chlorine atom.

i) Calcium (2,8,8,2)

ii) Chlorine (2,8,7)

c) Calcium chloride is an ionic compound. Explain how…

i) a calcium atom becomes a calcium ion.

ii) a chlorine atom becomes a chloride ion.

d) Draw an electron configuration diagram of calcium chloride ($CaCl_2$).

2 Calcium reacts with oxygen to form calcium oxide (CaO). Explain how the ionic bond is formed between calcium and oxygen to produce this compound.

Unit 2 – 12.1 & 12.2

The Covalent Bond

1 What, exactly, is a covalent bond?

_____

_____

2 The diagram represents a molecule of hydrogen chloride. It is a gas at room temperature.

a) What type of particles are represented by...

i) the dot (●): _____   **ii)** the crosses (**X**): _____

b) Explain why hydrogen chloride is a gas at room temperature.

_____

3 Nitrogen gas always consists of molecules made up of pairs of atoms, represented by N_2. Nitrogen atoms have five electrons in their outer shells.

a) Draw two individual nitrogen atoms.

b) Draw a pair of nitrogen atoms 'joined' to form an N_2 molecule.

a) b)

c) What sort of bond exists between the pair of atoms in part **b)**?

_____

d) Which are stronger – the bonds between nitrogen atoms within an N_2 molecule, or the forces of attraction between N_2 molecules?

_____

Covalent Bonding

4 Bromine atoms join together to form bromine molecules.

a) What is the name of the bond formed between the bromine atoms in a bromine molecule?

b) A bromine molecule can be represented in three ways:

    i) **Br – Br**   ii) Br Br   iii) Br Br

Use this information and your own knowledge, plus whatever information you need from the Periodic Table at the back of this book, to draw three structural representations for each substance in the table below.

Substance	Formula	Structural Formulae		
		i)	ii)	iii)
Chlorine	Cl_2			
Oxygen	O_2			
Ammonia	NH_3			
Hydrogen	H_2			
Water	H_2O			
Methane	CH_4			

Giant Covalent Structures

1 a) The diagrams show two giant structures of carbon: graphite and diamond.
Label the structures.

i)

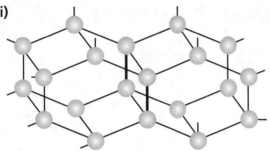

ii)

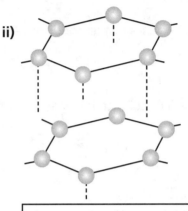

b) Explain the following:

i) Diamond has a very high melting point.

_____

_____

ii) Graphite conducts electricity.

_____

iii) Graphite can be used as a lubricant.

_____

_____

2 a) Silica (SiO_2) is a pure form of sand. Explain why it has a very high melting point.

_____

_____

b) Describe how the atoms in silica are bonded to each other.

_____

_____

Nanoparticles and Nanostructures

1 **a)** What is nanoscience the study of?

_____

b) One nanometre is 0.000000001m, i.e. one billionth of a metre. How else can it be written?

_____

c) Briefly describe the recent developments that have allowed scientists to see and control atoms at this dimension.

_____

_____

_____

_____

d) List two ways in which nanoparticles show different properties from the same materials in bulk.

i) _____

ii) _____

Nanocomposites

2 A lot of work has been done recently in the area of nanocomposite materials.

a) How do nanocomposite polymers differ from ordinary plastics?

_____

b) List four uses of nanocomposite materials.

i) _____

ii) _____

iii) _____

iv) _____

How Science Works

To answer the questions on this page, you will have to recall scientific facts and draw upon your knowledge of how science works, e.g. scientific procedures, issues and ideas.

1 a) Complete the table below, giving at least two uses for each example. The first box has been completed for you.

Substance	Properties	Uses
Metal	Strong / shiny / good conductor of heat and electricity / malleable (bendy).	Construction, jewellery, pans, wires, pipes
Non-metal	Brittle / insulator.	
Polymer	Lightweight / flexible / waterproof.	
Ionic compound	Hard / crystalline / soluble in water / high melting point / insulator when solid, but conducts electricity when molten or dissolved.	
Molecular covalent	Soft / low melting point / insulator.	
Macromolecules	Hard / high melting point.	
Nanomaterial	Very strong / huge surface area / conducts electricity.	
Smart material	Shape memory.	

b) Choose one substance from the table above. Suggest the type of structure it must have, based on its properties.

How Science Works

To answer the questions on this page, you will have to recall scientific facts and draw upon your knowledge of how science works, e.g. scientific procedures, issues and ideas.

1 a) Briefly describe what you understand by the following terms:

    i) nanomaterials

    ii) smart materials

b) List two industries in which nanomaterials could be used.

    i) .... **ii)** ....

c) List two industries in which smart materials could be used.

    i) .... **ii)** ....

2 Give one advantage and one disadvantage of using…

a) Nanomaterials   **i)** Advantage ....

                         ii) Disadvantage ....

b) Smart Materials   **i)** Advantage ....

                         ii) Disadvantage ....

Unit 2 – 12.3

Mass Number and Atomic Number

1 In the nucleus of a potassium atom there are 19 protons and 20 neutrons.

a) What is the mass number of potassium?

_____

b) What is the atomic number of potassium?

_____

c) How many electrons does an atom of potassium contain?

_____

d) Why is an atom of potassium neutral in terms of electronic charge?

_____

2 a) The letters A, B, C, D, E, F and G below represent seven different elements.

For each one write down **i)** the atomic number **ii)** the mass number **iii)** the number of protons and **iv)** the number of neutrons in one atom (A, B, C, D, E, F and G are not the chemical symbols).

	12 A 6	9 B 4	19 C 9	11 D 5	28 E 14	40 F 18	35 G 17
i) Atomic Number							
ii) Mass Number							
iii) No. of Protons							
iv) No. of Neutrons							

b) Use the periodic table at the back of this book to identify the elements A, B, C, D, E, F and G.

A = _____   B = _____   C = _____

D = _____   E = _____   F = _____

G = _____

Mass Number and Atomic Number

3 Complete the following table. The first one has been done for you.

	$^{14}_{7}\text{N}$	$^{197}_{79}\text{Au}$	$^{235}_{92}\text{U}$	Ca	$^{84}_{36}$	^{226}	$_{30}$	Fe
No. of Protons	7			20				26
No. of Neutrons	7			20			34	30
No. of Electrons	7					88		
Element	Nitrogen				Krypton			

Isotopes

4 What do we mean by the term **isotope**?

_____

5 The following are symbol representations of two isotopes of hydrogen.

i) $^{1}_{1}\text{H}$ ii) $^{2}_{1}\text{H}$

a) How do we know that they are isotopes of hydrogen?

_____

b) How many electrons would isotope **i)** contain?

_____

c) How many neutrons would isotope **ii)** contain?

_____

Unit 2 – 12.3

HT

Relative Atomic Mass (A$_r$)

1 Use the Periodic Table in at the back of this book to find out the relative atomic mass of each of the following elements:

a) Beryllium _____

b) Aluminium _____

c) Chlorine _____

d) Titanium _____

e) Bromine _____

f) Argon _____

g) Tellurium _____

h) Lithium _____

i) Tungsten _____

j) Francium _____

k) Nitrogen _____

l) Boron _____

Relative Formula Mass (M$_r$)

2 Calculate the relative formula mass of each of the following compounds. Use the Periodic Table at the back of this book to help you.

a) Water, H_2O _____

b) Sodium chloride, $NaCl$ _____

c) Copper oxide, CuO _____

d) Aluminium oxide, Al_2O_3 _____

e) Copper sulfate, $CuSO_4$ _____

f) Calcium hydroxide, $Ca(OH)_2$ _____

g) Aluminium chloride, $AlCl_3$ _____

h) Sulfuric acid, H_2SO_4 _____

i) Ethene, C_2H_4 _____

j) Sodium carbonate, Na_2CO_3 _____

k) Aluminium sulfate, $Al_2(SO_4)_3$ _____

l) Ammonia, NH_3 _____

3 For each of the following compounds, X represents an unknown element. The relative formula mass of the compound is given in brackets. Work out which element X represents.

a) XO (40) _____

b) XCl_2 (110) _____

c) CX_2 (44) _____

d) XNO_3 (63) _____

e) X_2 (62) _____

f) MgX_2 (94) _____

g) $X(OH)_2$ (171) _____

h) X_2O_3 (188) _____

© Letts and Lonsdale

Calculating Percentage Mass of an Element in a Compound

1 Using the periodic table at the back of this book, calculate the percentage mass of the given element in each of the compounds below.

a) Oxygen, O, in calcium oxide, CaO

b) Chlorine, Cl, in sodium chloride, NaCl

c) Calcium, Ca, in calcium carbonate, $CaCO_3$

d) Sulfur, S, in sulfur dioxide, SO_2

2 a) Use the Periodic Table at the back of this book to find the relative atomic mass of...

    i) hydrogen

    ii) sulfur

    iii) oxygen

b) Calculate the empirical formula of the compound formed by reacting 0.04g of hydrogen, 0.64g of sulfur and 1.28g of oxygen. Show your working.

Empirical formula:

The Mole

1 What do we mean by the term **mole** (mol)?

_____

_____

2 Use the Periodic Table at the back of this book to answer the following questions:

a) What is the molar mass (g/mol) of the following elements?

i) Calcium

_____

ii) Aluminium

_____

b) What is the mass (g) of one mole of the following compounds?

i) Sodium hydroxide (NaOH)

_____

ii) Sulfur dioxide (SO_2)

_____

3 **a)** What is the relationship used to calculate quantities involving moles?

_____

b) Use the relationship above and the Periodic Table (at the back of this book) to calculate…

i) the number of moles of calcium in 120g of the element.

_____

Answer: _____

ii) the number of moles of calcium carbonate ($CaCO_3$) in 500g of the compound.

_____

Answer: _____

Calculating the Mass of a Product

1 Calcium carbonate and hydrochloric acid react together to produce calcium chloride, carbon dioxide and water. Below is the balanced symbol equation for this reaction.

$$CaCO_{3(s)} + 2HCl_{(aq)} \longrightarrow CaCl_{2(aq)} + CO_{2(g)} + H_2O_{(l)}$$

a) Work out the M_r for each of the reactants and products shown in the equation, and write them below.

i) $CaCO_3$ _____   ii) $2HCl$ _____   iii) $CaCl_2$ _____

iv) CO_2 _____   v) H_2O _____

b) What is the total mass of all the reactants in the equation?

c) What is the total mass of all the products in the equation?

d) Would you have expected the masses in part **b)** and **c)** to be the same? Explain your answer.

e) What mass of calcium chloride can be produced from 2g of calcium carbonate?

Calculating the Mass of a Reactant

2 Referring to the equation in Question 1, how much calcium carbonate is needed to produce 1kg (1000g) of calcium chloride?

Calculating the Percentage Yield

1 Give three reasons why it is not always possible to obtain the full, calculated mass of a product from a reaction.

a) ....

b) ....

c) ....

HT

2 a) What is the term used to describe the actual quantity of product obtained through a reaction?

....

b) Write down the word equation that relates the actual amount of product obtained to the maximum amount of product that could theoretically be obtained.

$$\boxed{}$$

3 The reaction for making ammonia from hydrogen and nitrogen gas is shown by the following equation:

$$3H_2 + N_2 \longrightarrow 2NH_3$$

The industrial process for making ammonia produces 5.1 tonnes of ammonia from 6 tonnes of hydrogen gas. Calculate the percentage yield of this process.

....

....

Calculating Atom Economy

4 a) What is meant by the term **atom economy**?

....

....

b) What equation is used for calculating atom economy?

$$\boxed{}$$

Production of Ammonia – the Haber Process

1 a) The Haber Process is used to make ammonia. Complete this flow diagram of the process by filling in the spaces.

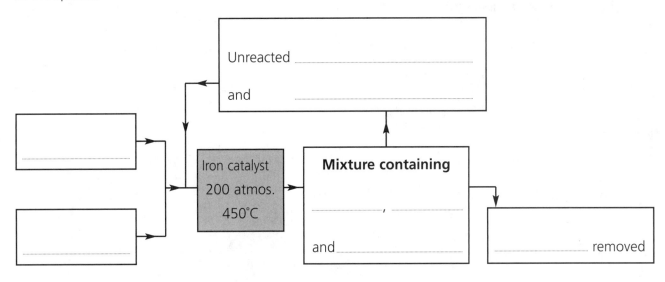

b) Write a word equation for the reaction (remember that the reaction is reversible!).

_____

c) Convert this to a balanced symbol equation, with state symbols.

_____

d) Where are the following raw materials obtained from?

i) Nitrogen: _____

ii) Hydrogen: _____

2 a) What is much of the ammonia produced by this process used for?

_____

b) What other substance is required for this purpose?

_____

How Science Works

HT

To answer the questions on this page, you will have to recall scientific facts and draw upon your knowledge of how science works, e.g. scientific procedures, issues and ideas.

1 Write a short definition for…

a) the relative atomic mass (A_r) of an element.

_____

_____

_____

b) the relative formula mass (M_r) of a compound.

_____

_____

_____

2 Write the word equation used to calculate atom economy.

Atom economy =

3 Sodium ethanoate has many industrial applications. For example, it is used in the production of some dyed textiles and leather goods. Below is the equation for the reaction:

Ethanoic acid + Sodium carbonate ⟶ Sodium ethanoate + Carbon dioxide + Water

$$C_2H_4O_2 + Na_2CO_3 \longrightarrow C_2H_3NaO_2 + CO_2 + H_2O$$

a) Calculate the atom economy of this reaction (you will have to balance the equation first).

b) What is the percentage of waste products in this reaction?

_____

Rates of Reactions

1 a) What is the term used to describe the minimum amount of energy required to cause a chemical reaction?

....

b) What are the four main factors which affect the rate of reaction?

i) ....

ii) ....

iii) ....

iv) ....

Temperature of the Reactants

2 The word equation below shows the reaction between lumps of calcium carbonate and hydrochloric acid.

Calcium carbonate + Hydrochloric acid ⟶ Calcium chloride + Water + Carbon dioxide

The rate of reaction can be studied by measuring the amount of carbon dioxide gas produced. The graph shows the result of four experiments: A, B, C and D. For each experiment, only the temperature of the acid was changed.

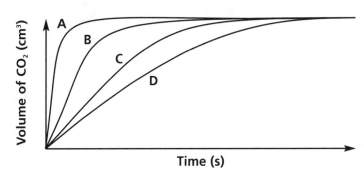

a) What must be kept constant in order to make the experiment a fair test?

....

b) Which graph line shows the results of the experiment with the acid at the highest temperature?

....

c) Explain your answer to part **b)** fully in terms of the particles involved.

....

....

....

Unit 2 – 12.4

Concentration of the Dissolved Reactants

1 A student carried out an experiment where hydrochloric acid was reacted with sodium thiosulfate. In this reaction, a yellow precipitate of sulfur is formed. The rate of reaction can be measured by timing how long it takes a cross drawn under a flask to disappear from view. The results obtained are shown in the table below:

Concentration of Acid (M)	Time Taken for Cross to Disappear (s)
0.1	60
0.2	40
0.4	24
0.6	13
0.8	8
1.0	4

a) Plot a graph of the results on the axes below.

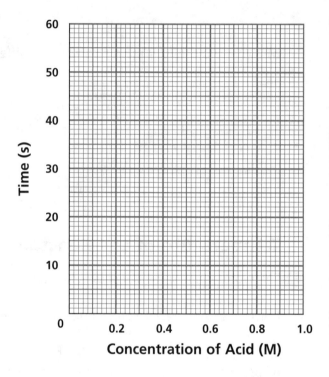

b) i) What happens to the rate of reaction as the concentration increases?

_____

ii) Explain your answer to part **b) i)** in terms of the particles involved.

_____

_____

HT

2 How are concentrations of solutions measured?

_____

3 a) What happens to the rate of reaction when the pressure on a gas increases?

_____

b) Explain your answer in terms of the particles involved.

_____

_____

Surface Area of Solid Reactants

1 Large particles have a small surface area in relation to their volume, and small particles have a large surface area in relation to their volume.

Explain how the size of the particles involved affects the rate of reaction.

....

....

....

Using a Catalyst

2 What is a catalyst?

....

....

3 The word equation below shows the decomposition of hydrogen peroxide to give water and oxygen.

Hydrogen peroxide ⟶ Water + Oxygen

Adding manganese (IV) oxide speeds up this reaction without altering the products formed.

A student adds 2g of manganese (IV) oxide to 100cm³ of hydrogen peroxide at 20°C. He measures the volume of oxygen produced over a period of 5 minutes. The results are shown in the table alongside:

Time (mins)	0	1	2	3	4	5
Total Volume of Oxygen (cm³)	0	54	82	96	100	100

a) Suggest what the total volume of oxygen would be after 6 minutes. Explain your answer.

....

....

b) Explain how manganese (IV) oxide increases the rate of the reaction.

....

Unit 2 – 12.4

Analysing the Rate of Reaction

1 a) Describe how the rate of a chemical reaction can be found.

_____

_____

b) Write the general equation that can be used to calculate the rate of reaction.

_____

_____

2 The graph below shows the results of an investigation into the reaction of magnesium with dilute hydrochloric acid.

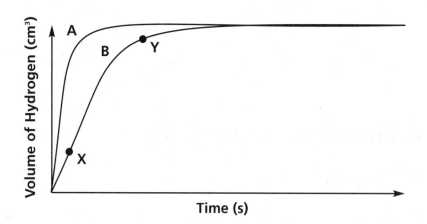

a) Complete the word equation for the reaction.

Magnesium + Hydrochloric acid ⟶ _____ + Hydrogen

b) Which graph line shows the fastest rate of reaction?

_____

c) For Graph B, is the rate of reaction greatest at X or Y?

_____

d) Give three possible reasons why the rate of reaction is different for Graphs A and B.

i) _____

ii) _____

iii) _____

How Science Works

To answer the questions on this page, you will have to recall scientific facts and draw upon your knowledge of how science works, e.g. scientific procedures, issues and ideas.

1 What four factors affect the rate of reaction?

a) ....

b) ....

c) ....

d) ....

2 The decomposition of hydrogen peroxide to give water and oxygen is shown below as a word equation:

Hydrogen peroxide ⟶ Water + Oxygen

A student adds 2g of manganese (IV) oxide (a catalyst) to 100cm³ of hydrogen peroxide at 20°C. He measured the volume of oxygen produced over a period of 5 minutes. The results are shown in the table alongside:

Time (mins)	0	1	2	3	4	5
Total Volume of Oxygen (cm³)	0	54	82	96	100	100

a) Plot the results on the graph paper alongside. Label this Graph A.

b) The student repeats the experiment. This time he adds 2g of manganese oxide to a mixture of 50cm³ of hydrogen peroxide and 50cm³ of water at 20°C.

i) On the same axes, sketch the graph that you would expect if all other conditions were kept the same as in the first experiment. Label this Graph B.

ii) Briefly explain the difference between Graphs A and B.

....

....

....

....

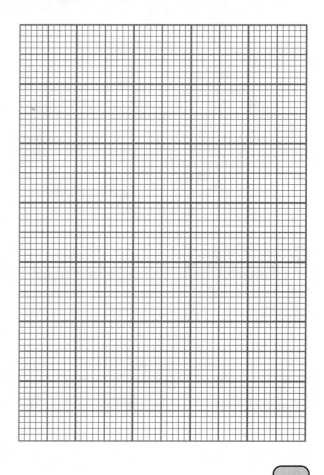

How Science Works

To answer the questions on this page, you will have to recall scientific facts and draw upon your knowledge of how science works, e.g. scientific procedures, issues and ideas.

1 Why can catalysts be used over and over again?

....

....

2 List three transition materials that are used as catalysts in industrial processes.

a) ....

b) ....

c) ....

3 Why are nanomaterials ideal for use as industrial catalysts?

....

4 a) List three advantages of using catalysts in industrial processes.

i) ....

ii) ....

iii) ....

b) List two disadvantages of using catalysts in industrial processes.

i) ....

ii) ....

5 Use the library, Internet or another secondary source to find one example of a catalyst being used effectively in industry. Summarise your findings below.

....

....

....

....

....

Exothermic Reactions

1 Methane reacts with oxygen to produce carbon dioxide and water.

a) Write a word equation for this reaction.

_____

b) What is the name given to a reaction that gives out heat?

_____

c) What else is produced in addition to the compounds mentioned in this question?

_____

d) In an exothermic reaction, what happens to the yield if the temperature…

i) rises? _____   **ii)** falls? _____

Endothermic Reactions

2 When ammonium chloride is dissolved in water, an endothermic reaction takes place.

a) What is an **endothermic reaction**?

_____

b) In an endothermic reaction, what happens to the yield if the temperature…

i) rises? _____   **ii)** falls? _____

3 a) What substance is produced when hydrated copper sulfate crystals are gently heated?

_____

b) The change is reversible. What does this mean?

_____

c) Would the reverse reaction be endothermic or exothermic?

_____

Reversible Reactions

1 The diagram below shows an experiment where ammonium chloride is heated.

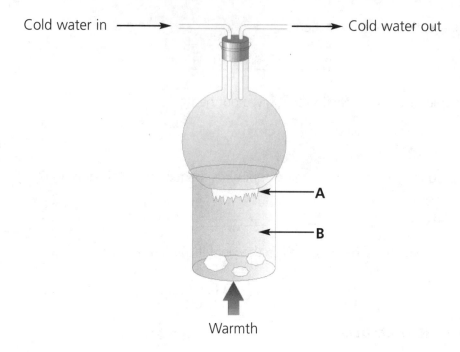

Cold water in ⟶ ⟶ Cold water out

A

B

Warmth

The word equation for the reaction is:

Ammonium chloride ⇌ Ammonia + Hydrogen chloride

a) What does the symbol ⇌ mean?

....

b) Explain why…

i) ammonium chloride is found at point A.

....

....

ii) ammonia and hydrogen chloride gas are found in the beaker at point B.

....

....

c) Write a symbol equation for this reaction.

....

Reversible Reactions in Closed Systems

HT

1. In the Haber Process, two gases, nitrogen and hydrogen, react together to produce ammonia in a reversible reaction. The table below shows how the yield of ammonia changes at different temperatures and pressures.

The symbol equation is: $N_{2(g)} + 3H_{2(g)} \rightleftharpoons 2NH_{3(g)}$

Pressure (atmospheres)	Percentage Yield of Ammonia at 300°C	Percentage Yield of Ammonia at 600°C
100	43	4
200	62	12
300	74	18
400	79	19
500	80	20

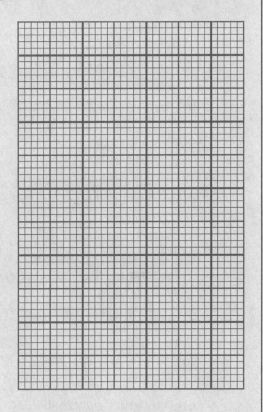

a) Plot a graph of the data above.

b) Is this an endothermic or exothermic reaction?

_____

c) i) Explain why the yield of ammonia is affected by increasing the pressure at a constant temperature.

_____

_____

_____

ii) Explain how the yield of ammonia is affected by decreasing the temperature at a constant pressure.

_____

_____

_____

d) To reach equilibrium, the gases must be in a closed system. Why is this?

_____

Effect of Varying Conditions on Reversible Reactions

1 a) In the Haber Process, a mixture of nitrogen and hydrogen is passed over iron at a temperature of about 450°C and a pressure of 200 atmospheres.

    i) Write down a word and symbol equation for the reaction.

_____

    ii) Explain why the nitrogen and hydrogen are passed over iron.

_____

b) The graph alongside shows how temperature and pressure affect the percentage yield of ammonia in the reaction.

    i) From looking at the graph, which combination of temperature and pressure gives the highest yield?

_____

_____

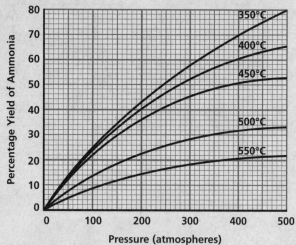

    ii) Why is this combination of temperature and pressure not used in the commercial production of ammonia?

_____

_____

A Compromise Solution

2 a) Why is ammonia produced at a temperature of 450°C and a pressure of 200 atmospheres?

_____

b) Use the graph to find the yield that this combination of temperature and pressure gives.

_____

c) What happens to the hydrogen and nitrogen that has not reacted to produce ammonia?

_____

How Science Works

To answer the questions on this page, you will have to recall scientific facts and draw upon your knowledge of how science works, e.g. scientific procedures, issues and ideas.

1 a) Why do energy requirements need to be considered when using chemical reactions in industrial processes?

....

....

....

b) With reference to chemical reactions being used in industrial processes, name one other factor that needs to be considered that can affect…

i) how economical a process is.

....

ii) how environmentally friendly the process is.

....

2 a) What two main variables affect the speed of a chemical reaction in an industrial process?

i) .... **ii)** ....

b) List two advantages and two disadvantages for variable i) above.

Advantages   **i)** ....

              ii) ....

Disdvantages **iii)** ....

              iv) ....

c) List two advantages and two disadvantages for variable ii) in part a) above.

Advantages   **i)** ....

              ii) ....

Disdvantages **iii)** ....

              iv) ....

Principles of Electrolysis

1 What are ionic substances?

....

....

....

2 In terms of elements and ions, explain what electrolysis is.

....

....

....

3 a) Fill in the type of charge (i.e. **positive** or **negative**) to complete these two sentences, which describe what happens during electrolysis.

   i) Ions with a .... charge move towards the positive electrode.

   ii) Ions with a .... charge move towards the negative electrode.

b) If there is a mixture of ions in a solution during electrolysis, what is the formation of the products dependent on?

....

4 Which two elements would be produced through the electrolysis of copper chloride solution? Give the correct state symbols to indicate the state of these products.

a) i) Element: .... **ii)** State symbol: ....

b) i) Element: .... **ii)** State symbol: ....

Redox Reactions

5 Alongside each statement below, write whether the process being described is **reduction** or **oxidation**.

a) Positively charged ions gain electrons. ....

b) Negatively charged ions lose electrons. ....

6 Complete this mnemonic to help you remember what occurs in a redox reaction.

a) O .... I .... L ....

b) R .... I .... G ....

Purification of Copper by Electrolysis

1 Copper which is used for electrical wiring must be very pure. Pure copper can be made by electrolysis. The diagram alongside shows a very simple arrangement.

a) For the electrolysis of copper to take place, what must the solution in the cell contain?

....

b) Which electrode should be made of impure copper?

....

c) Which electrode should be made of pure copper? ....

d) Which electrode increases in size during electrolysis? ....

e) Which electrode decreases in size during electrolysis? ....

f) Explain, in terms of ions, why the two electrodes change in size during electrolysis.

....

....

....

....

....

HT **2 a)** Write a half-equation to show what happens at the negative electrode during electrolysis.

....

b) Write a half-equation to show what happens at the positive electrode during electrolysis.

....

Industrial Electrolysis of Sodium Chloride Solution

1 The diagram alongside shows the arrangement for the electrolysis of a solution of sodium chloride.

Sodium chloride solution NaCl

Positive electrode

Membrane

Negative electrode

a) Why must sodium chloride be in solution for electrolysis to take place?

....

b) i) Name the gas formed at the negative electrode.

....

ii) Name the gas formed at the positive electrode.

....

c) Describe a test for the gas formed at the positive electrode.

....

d) Apart from the two gases, what else is produced during the electrolysis of sodium chloride?

....

2 For each reagent produced, give one example of how it can be used commercially.

a) Reagent: .... Use: ....

b) Reagent: .... Use: ....

c) Reagent: .... Use: ....

Indicators

3 a) What is an indicator?

....

....

b) Name two indicators.

i) .... **ii)** ....

Neutralisation

1 A beaker containing 100cm³ of sodium hydroxide had universal indicator solution added to it. Sulfuric acid was then added using a burette and the pH of the solution was estimated by gauging the colour of the liquid. The solution was constantly stirred. The results are shown in the table below:

Volume of Acid Added (cm³)	0	4	12	30	50
pH of Solution	14	12	10	8	7

a) Plot a graph of these results on the paper provided.

b) What colour was the solution at the start?

_____

c) What colour was the solution at the end?

_____

d) Write a symbol equation for the reaction taking place.

_____

e) What is the name given to this type of reaction?

_____

f) Describe the reaction in terms of ions.

_____

g) Write an equation for the reaction showing the ions that combine.

_____

2 Ammonium nitrate and ammonium sulfate can be used as fertilisers.

a) Ammonia is reacted with an acid in each case. Write word equations for the formation of…

i) ammonium nitrate: _____

ii) ammonium sulfate: _____

b) What is the name given to these types of reaction?

_____

Soluble Salts from Metals

1 a) Write a word equation for the general reaction that takes place between a metal and dilute acid.

....

b) Describe what is meant by the term **salt**.

....

....

c) Indicate what happens when each of the metals alongside are reacted with an acid. The first one has been completed for you.

Metal	Reaction
i) Zinc	Fairly reasonable
ii) Silver	
iii) Magnesium	
iv) Potassium	

Soluble Salts from Insoluble Bases

2 What is the difference between a base and an alkali?

....

3 Explain, using diagrams, how you would obtain crystals of the salt formed in the reaction between copper oxide and hydrochloric acid.

Step 1:	Step 2:	Step 3:

4 The substance produced when ammonia is dissolved in water can be neutralised with acids to produce ammonium salts, which are important as alkalis.

What is the substance produced when ammonia is dissolved in water?

....

Salts of Alkali Metals

1 a) To refresh your memory, write a word equation to summarise what happens in a neutralisation reaction.

....

b) Complete the word equations for the following reactions:

i)   Iron hydroxide   +   Sulfuric acid   ⟶   ....   +   Water

ii)   ....   + ...   ⟶   Calcium sulfate   +   Water

iii)   Potassium hydroxide   + ...   ⟶   Potassium nitrate   + ...

iv)   ....   +   Hydrochloric acid   ⟶   Sodium chloride   + ...

v)   ....   + ...   ⟶   Calcium chloride   +   Water

vi)   Copper oxide   +   Hydrochloric acid   ⟶   ....   + ...

vii)   ....   +   Nitric acid   ⟶   Sodium nitrate   + ...

viii)   ....   + ...   ⟶   Sodium sulfate   + ...

ix)   Zinc oxide   +   Nitric acid   ⟶   ....   + ...

x)   Ammonia   + ...   ⟶   Ammonium chloride   + ...

Insoluble Salts

2 a) How are insoluble salts made?

....

....

....

b) Describe one practical application of this process.

....

....

....

How Science Works

To answer the questions on this page, you will have to recall scientific facts and draw upon your knowledge of how science works, e.g. scientific procedures, issues and ideas.

1 a) Under what circumstances can ionic substances conduct electricity and be broken down?

....

b) What process uses electrical energy to break down these substances?

....

c) In this process, what is another name for…

i) the positive electrode? ....

ii) the negative electrode? ....

2 List the three main rules for predicting the results of electrolysing ionic solutions.

a) ....

....

b) ....

....

c) ....

....

3 Through electrolysis, concentrated hydrochloric acid gives equal volumes of hydrogen and chlorine gas.

Hydrochloric acid $\longrightarrow$ Hydrogen + Chlorine

Write and balance half-equations which represent the changes that occur at the two electrodes during this electrolysis.

a) i) Equation: ....

ii) At which electrode? ....

b) i) Equation: ....

ii) At which electrode? ....

How Science Works

To answer the questions on this page, you will have to recall scientific facts and draw upon your knowledge of how science works, e.g. scientific procedures, issues and ideas.

4 a) Briefly explain the process of electrolysis.

b) Why is electrolysis important industrially?

5 a) Write a word equation for the electrolysis of sea water (i.e. brine).

b) List three advantages of this process.

   i)

   ii)

   iii)

c) List three disadvantages of this process.

   i)

   ii)

   iii)

d) Using your lists of advantages and disadvantages, briefly evaluate the long-term impact of this process on the environment.

How Science Works

To answer the questions on this page, you will have to recall scientific facts and draw upon your knowledge of how science works, e.g. scientific procedures, issues and ideas.

1 a) What are the two main groups of salts?

   i) ....   **ii)** ....

b) Complete the following sentences.

   i) Insoluble salts are made from ....

   ii) Two solutions of soluble salts can react to make ....

2 List the five rules which define the solubility of salts.

   a) ....

   b) ....

   c) ....

   d) ....

   e) ....

3 Complete the following table:

Acid	Salt Products
Hydrochloric acid	....
....	Sulfates
Nitric acid	....

4 a) i) Write a general word equation for the production of insoluble salts.

   ....

   ii) Write a specific word equation for the production of copper sulfate.

   ....

b) Briefly explain how copper sulfate is produced.

   ....

   ....

   ....

1 Alongside each definition, write the word or phrase that is being described.

a) 4 letters   **i)** A compound that has a pH value lower than 7.   ....

                   ii) The molecular mass of a substance expressed in grams.   ....

                   iii) The product of a chemical reaction between a base and an acid.   ....

b) 5 letters   The amount of a product obtained from a reaction.   ....

c) 6 letters   **i)** A compound that has a pH value higher than 7.   ....

                   ii) A positively charged particle found in the nucleus of atoms.   ....

d) 7 letters   **i)** A neutrally charged particle found in the nucleus of atoms.   ....

                   ii) The small central core of an atom.   ....

e) 8 letters   **i)** Elements in Group 7 of the Periodic Table.   ....

                   ii) Inert, colourless gases. (2 words)   ....

                   iii) A negatively charged particle found outside the nucleus of an atom.   ....

f) 9 letters   **i)** A reaction involving the gain of oxygen or the loss of hydrogen.   ....

                   ii) A reaction involving the loss of oxygen or the gain of hydrogen.   ....

g) 10 letters   Pieces of metal or carbon which allow electric current to enter and leave during electrolysis.   ....

h) 11 letters   **i)** The state in which a chemical reaction proceeds at the same rate as its reverse reaction.   ....

                   ii) The sum of the atomic masses of all atoms in a molecule. (2 words)   ....

i) 12 letters   **i)** Elements in Group 1 of the Periodic Table. (2 words)   ....

                   ii) The number of an element's place in the Periodic Table; the number of protons an element has in the nucleus of its atom. (2 words)   ....

                   iii) The process by which an electric current flowing through a liquid containing ions causes the liquid to undergo chemical decomposition.   ....

                   iv) The process of two or more atoms losing or gaining electrons to become charged ions. (2 words)   ....

j) 13 letters   **i)** Materials with a very small grain size.   ....

                   ii) The removal of a solid from a solution.   ....

k) 14 letters   **i)** Reaction between an acid and a base which forms a neutral solution.   ....

                   ii) Materials that have one or more properties that can be altered. (2 words)   ....

l) 15 letters   A bond between two atoms in which both atoms share one electron. (2 words)   ....

m) 18 letters   **i)** A reaction which gives off heat. (2 words)   ....

                   ii) A reaction in which products react to reform the original reactants. (2 words)   ....

n) 19 letters   A reaction which takes in heat from the surroundings. (2 words)   ....

Unit 2 – Key Words

2 Complete this wordsearch to find all your answers to Question 1.

E	J	A	L	K	A	L	I	M	E	T	A	L	S	K	T	B	N	S
B	N	O	E	F	T	U	F	O	R	M	U	L	A	M	A	S	S	A
S	A	D	X	I	E	L	E	C	T	R	O	N	Y	S	T	A	H	L
M	N	U	O	P	R	E	C	I	P	I	T	A	T	I	O	N	L	T
A	O	R	T	T	H	A	L	O	G	E	N	S	Y	S	M	Q	G	M
R	M	N	H	N	H	A	Y	I	E	L	D	N	A	Y	I	V	N	T
T	A	N	E	B	A	E	X	T	V	Y	R	O	N	L	C	N	I	D
M	T	O	R	N	T	N	R	E	D	U	C	T	I	O	N	M	D	A
A	E	I	M	U	O	P	Z	M	H	Y	B	O	P	R	U	T	N	M
T	R	T	I	C	M	I	R	T	I	N	A	R	R	T	M	A	O	C
E	I	A	C	L	I	L	T	B	T	C	B	P	A	C	B	S	B	Y
R	A	D	R	E	C	A	U	A	I	M	R	V	C	E	E	X	T	J
I	L	I	E	U	M	K	C	D	S	Q	N	E	T	L	R	Z	N	N
A	S	X	A	S	A	L	L	O	P	I	W	R	A	E	H	B	E	E
L	Z	O	C	G	S	A	B	S	U	R	L	R	T	C	N	R	L	U
S	Y	A	T	D	S	N	O	B	L	E	G	A	S	T	T	A	A	T
K	M	U	I	R	B	I	L	I	U	Q	E	W	R	R	K	I	V	R
G	S	M	O	M	O	L	P	D	R	X	Y	B	J	T	K	T	O	O
R	I	O	N	I	C	B	O	N	D	I	N	G	D	N	U	D	C	N
S	O	E	L	E	C	T	R	O	D	E	S	H	M	O	L	E	Y	K
R	E	V	E	R	S	I	B	L	E	R	E	A	C	T	I	O	N	U

The Periodic Table

1 The diagram alongside shows an outline of the Periodic Table.

Using only the elements shown, answer the following questions:

a) Write the name and symbol of...

   i) a metal ....   **ii)** a non-metal ....

b) Write the name and symbol of **i)** a metal and **ii)** a non-metal in the same **period**.

   i) ....   **ii)** ....

c) Write the name and symbol of **i)** a metal and **ii)** a non-metal in the same **group**.

   i) ....   **ii)** ....

d) Why is it better to arrange the elements in terms of their electronic structure and not in order of their relative atomic masses?

....

....

....

e) Lithium and sodium are in Group 1 of the Periodic Table. They have similar chemical properties. Explain, in terms of their atomic structure, why they have similar properties.

....

Early Attempts to Classify the Elements

2 **a)** Describe two ways in which John Newlands' arrangement of the Periodic Table was different from the modern Periodic Table.

....

....

b) Dimitri Mendeleev developed Newlands' Periodic Table. Describe the work of Mendeleev that brought us closer to today's Periodic Table.

....

....

Group 1 – The Alkali Metals

1 Lithium is an element in Group 1 of the Periodic Table. A piece of lithium is placed onto some water. The water has universal indicator in it.

a) Why does the lithium float?

b) What happens to the lithium?

c) Write a word equation for the reaction that takes place between lithium and water.

d) The colour of the water turns from green to purple. Explain why this happens.

e) Name two other elements in Group 1 of the Periodic Table. For each one, describe how they would react with water (compare your answer to the description you gave for lithium above).

i) Element: _____   Reaction with water: _____

ii) Element: _____   Reaction with water: _____

f) Lithium fluoride can be made by reacting lithium with fluorine gas. Write a word equation for the reaction.

g) This reaction produces hydrogen gas.

i) How would you test for this gas?

ii) What result would you expect if hydrogen was present?

2 a) Briefly describe what happens when alkali metals react with non-metals.

b) Write a word equation for the reaction of sodium (alkali metal) with chlorine (a non-metal).

Group 7 – Halogens

1 Fluorine and chlorine are both elements found in Group 7 of the Periodic Table.

a) Write down the chemical symbol for…

i) chlorine gas _____   **ii)** fluorine gas _____

b) What else have fluorine and chlorine got in common? Suggest at least four things.

_____

_____

2 Use a tick (✓) or a cross (✗) to indicate whether the following statements about the elements of Group 7 are true or false.

a) They have coloured vapours. ☐   **b)** They are good conductors of heat. ☐

c) They exist as single atoms. ☐   **d)** They are poor conductors of electricity. ☐

e) They are crumbly when solid. ☐   **f)** They have low boiling and melting points. ☐

3 Use the Periodic Table at the back of this book to help you draw electron configurations for each of the following halogens, use rings to represent electron shells, and dots or crosses to represent the electrons.

i) Chlorine atom   **ii)** Chloride ion   **iii)** Fluorine atom   **iv)** Fluoride ion

4 A student carried out an experiment to see how halogens react with other halogen compounds. He added aqueous solutions of bromine, iodine and chlorine, in turn, to aqueous solutions of sodium iodide, sodium chloride and sodium bromide.

	Sodium Iodide (NaI)	Sodium Chloride (NaCl)	Sodium Bromide (NaBr)
Bromine			
Iodine			
Chlorine			

Complete the table of results alongside by writing **reaction** or **no reaction** for each combination.

Unit 3 – 13.1

Trends in Group 1 and Trends in Group 7

HT

1 Explain, in terms of electron arrangement, why the metals in Group 1 have similar properties.

2 Draw dots or crosses onto the rings in the two boxes to show the electron configurations of the two metals.

a) Sodium (11 electrons)

b) Potassium (19 electrons)

a)

b)

3 Explain why potassium is more reactive than sodium.

4 Refer back to your electron configuration drawings of chlorine and fluorine atoms on the previous page.

a) Why is the behaviour (properties) of these elements similar to each other?

b) In what way would they be different? Explain your answer.

Transition Metals

5 a) Give the names of five transition metals.

i) _____ ii) _____ iii) _____

iv) _____ v) _____

b) List four properties that these metals have in common.

i) _____ ii) _____

iii) _____ iv) _____

© Letts and Lonsdale

How Science Works

To answer the questions on this page, you will have to recall scientific facts and draw upon your knowledge of how science works, e.g. scientific procedures, issues and ideas.

1 a) Use a line to connect each of the scientists below to the correct theory or research.

| Mendeleev | Divided the elements into groups of three, in which all three elements had very similar properties. He found that there was a pattern to the atomic weights of the elements in each group. | ☐ |

| Döbereiner | Arranged all the elements into the order of their atomic weight and discovered that every eighth element appeared to have similar properties. | ☐ |

| John Newlands | Proposed that all substances were made of tiny building blocks of the same basic material, called atoms. | ☐ |

| Democritus | Arranged all the elements in the order of their atomic weight, and left spaces for elements that had yet to be discovered. | ☐ |

| John Dalton | Suggested that the atoms of a particular element were all the same, and that these were rearranged when chemical changes took place. | ☐ |

b) Now number each of the pairs above from **1** to **5**, to show the order in which these events occurred.

2 John Newlands' work played an important role in the development of the Periodic Table. However, his conclusions were flawed. Give two reasons for these flaws.

a) ....

b) ....

3 What is the main difference between Mendeleev's Periodic Table and the modern Periodic Table?

....

4 Some recently discovered elements are radioactive and have a very short lifespan. Explain how it is possible to make predictions about their chemical properties without being able to study them thoroughly.

....

....

Unit 3 – 13.2

Acids and Alkalis

1 a) What type of ions are responsible for the characteristics of acids? Write the name and the chemical symbol.

b) What type of ions are responsible for the characteristics of alkalis (or bases)? Write the written name and the chemical symbol.

2 Fill in the missing words to complete the following two sentences about acids and alkalis.

a) An acid is a proton _____.

b) A base is a proton _____.

3 a) How are acids and alkalis classified?

b) What determines the strength of an acid or alkali?

4 a) A scientist has two beakers of hydrochloric acid in solution. The solution in Beaker A has a high concentration. The solution in Beaker B has a low concentration. Which solution will have the highest pH?

b) Explain the reason for your answer to part a).

c) What units are used to measure concentration? Give your answer in words and then give the correct abbreviation.

d) Apart from pH, what other factor can be used to find the strength of an acid?

Titration

1 What is titration? _____

2 Number the following stages **1** to **7**, to show the order in which they should be carried out for a titration. Remember, you must know the concentration of either the acid or the alkali.

a) Fill the burette with acid and take an initial reading of the volume. ☐

b) Wash and rinse the pipette with the alkali that is to be used. ☐

c) Carefully add the acid to the alkali until the indicator changes to show the solution is pH neutral. ☐

d) Wash and rinse a burette in the acid that is to be used. ☐

e) Calculate the volume of acid used to neutralise the alkali. ☐

f) Add a suitable indicator to the alkali. ☐

g) Use the pipette to measure an accurate volume of alkali and transfer it to a conical flask. ☐

3 Suggest a suitable indicator for each of the following combinations.

a) strong acid + strong alkali _____

HT **b)** strong acid + weak alkali _____

4 Write a word equation and a symbol equation to show what happens when neutralisation takes place.

a) Word equation: _____

b) Symbol equation: _____

HT **5 a)** What is the formula for calculating the concentration of a solution?

Concentration of solution =

b) A titration is carried out and $0.05dm^3$ of hydrochloric acid neutralises $0.3dm^3$ of potassium hydroxide of concentration $0.5mol\ dm^{-3}$. The equation for the neutralisation is **HCl + KOH ⟶ KCl + H$_2$O**. Calculate the concentration of the hydrochloric acid.

How Science Works

To answer the questions on this page, you will have to recall scientific facts and draw upon your knowledge of how science works, e.g. scientific procedures, issues and ideas.

1 In 1887 Arrhenius proposed that…

- all acids release hydrogen ions when they are dissolved in water
- alkalis (soluble bases) form hydroxide ions in water
- molecules ionise in water.

a) Give two reasons why these proposals are very restrictive.

i) _____

ii) _____

b) Suggest one reason why Arrhenius's work was not immediately accepted by the scientific community.

_____

_____

2 a) List the three key points that Lowry and Brønsted identified, which underpin our current understanding of how acids and alkalis behave.

i) _____

ii) _____

iii) _____

b) How is this research an improvement on Arrhenius's work?

_____

_____

c) By the time Lowry and Brønsted announced their research, the scientific community had a better understanding of atomic structure. Why might this have helped their research to be accepted more quickly than Arrhenius's was?

_____

_____

d) Lowry and Brønsted worked independently but produced the same conclusions. Why might this have helped their research to be accepted more quickly than Arrhenius's was?

_____

© Letts and Lonsdale

The Importance of Water

1 Why is water an essential natural resource?

2 Suggest two additional practical uses of water.

a)

b)

The Water Cycle

3 Number the following descriptions **1** to **6**, to show the sequence of events that make up the water cycle.

a) As the water vapour rises into the atmosphere it cools.

b) Rainwater drains off the land into rivers, which flow to the sea.

c) The clouds rise higher in the atmosphere.

d) The water droplets grow larger and fall as rain.

e) Condensation produces clouds formed from water droplets.

f) Heat energy from the Sun causes water in rivers, lakes and oceans to evaporate.

4 Describe briefly how snow is formed.

Drinking Water

5 a) Name two ways in which water is prepared to make it safe for drinking.

i)

ii)

b) How can further dissolved substances be removed from tap water?

Dissolving Substances in Water

1 Use the words **solvent** and **solute** to complete these two sentences about dissolving substances.

a) A solid that dissolves in water is called a ....

b) When a solid is dissolved in water, the water is called a ....

Solubility of Compounds

2 a) In terms of solubility, what is the difference between ionic compounds and covalent compounds?

....

....

b) What effect does the temperature of the solvent usually have on the solubility of a compound?

....

c) What unit of measurement is used to describe the solubility of a substance?

....

3 Alongside is a typical solubility curve for copper sulfate water.

a) From the graph, find the maximum amount of copper sulfate that dissolves in water at...

i) 40°C. ....

ii) 80°C. ....

b) If a saturated solution of copper sulfate cools down from 80°C to 40°C, what quantity of copper sulfate per 100g of water will crystallise out?

....

....

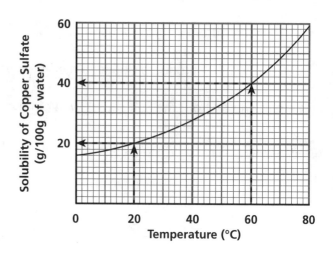

Solubility of Gases

4 a) Name two common water-soluble gases.

i) .... **ii)** ....

b) What two factors can increase the solubility of a water-soluble gas?

i) ....

ii) ....

Hard and Soft Water

1 a) Explain why the tap water in some areas of the UK is harder than in other areas.

b) Name one advantage of living in a hard water area.

c) Name one disadvantage of living in a hard water area.

2 a) In terms of ions, explain how adding washing soda can **soften** hard water.

b) Write a word equation and symbol equation to show the reaction that takes place in part a).

    i) Word equation:

    ii) Symbol equation:

3 Hard water can also be **softened** by passing it through an ion-exchange column. The column contains a special resin which supplies hydrogen ions, H^+, or sodium ions, Na^+.

a) Explain how this helps to soften the water.

b) Why does the resin need to be replaced regularly?

How Science Works

To answer the questions on this page, you will have to recall scientific facts and draw upon your knowledge of how science works, e.g. scientific procedures, issues and ideas.

1 Is it safe to drink tap water in the UK?

....

2 Name two of the organisations responsible for monitoring the quality of drinking water.

a) ....

b) ....

3 a) Suggest three causes of water pollution.

   i) ....

   ii) ....

   iii) ....

b) Is there a common link between the causes you listed above? If so, what is it?

   ....

c) In terms of health, why is water pollution a problem?

   ....

d) In terms of the environment, why is water pollution a problem?

   ....

   ....

4 a) In the UK, sales of bottled water have increased dramatically over the past five years. Suggest two reasons why people in the UK might prefer to drink bottled water rather than tap water.

   i) ....

   ii) ....

b) In the UK, some companies that produce bottled water describe their product as 'pure'. Is this an accurate description? Explain your answer.

   ....

   ....

   ....

Joules and Calories

1 a) What term is used to describe a chemical reaction that...

i) gives out heat energy? ....

ii) takes in heat energy? ....

b) State the unit of measurement for energy. Give the full written name and the correct abbreviation.

....

c) What name is given to the amount of energy required to heat up 1g of water by 1°C?

....

d) Explain what happens if the amount of energy consumed by an animal or human is greater than the amount of energy used (through respiration, movement, etc.).

....

....

Measuring Energy

2 A student carried out an investigation to find the amount of energy in one peanut. He placed 100g of water in a calorimeter and ignited the peanut beneath it. The table below shows the mass of the peanut and the temperature of the water before and after the peanut was burnt.

	Before	After
Mass of Peanut	0.3g	0.1g
Temperature of 100g of Water	18°C	28°C

a) What is the total change in mass of the peanut in this investigation? ....

b) What is the total change in temperature of 100g of water in this investigation? ....

c) If it takes 4.2 joules of energy to raise the temperature of 1g of water by 1°C, calculate the amount of energy 1g of peanut will produce, using the information above.

....

....

....

....

Making and Breaking Bonds

1 **a)** In terms of the bonds between atoms and moleclues, describe what happens during a chemical reaction.

_____

_____

b) **i)** In terms of the bonds between atoms, what type of change requires a lot of energy?

_____

ii) What is the name given to processes that require energy?

_____

c) **i)** In terms of the bonds between atoms, what type of change produces a lot of energy?

_____

ii) What is the name given to processes that produce energy?

_____

Energy Level Diagrams

2 In the space provided, sketch an energy level diagram to show the energy change that takes place in…

a) the type of reaction described in Question 1, part b).

b) the type of reaction described in Question 1, part c).

a)

b)

3 The energy level diagram alongside shows the activation energy needed to start a particular reaction. In the box alongside, sketch an energy level diagram for the same reaction if a catalyst was introduced.

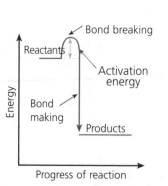

© Letts and Lonsdale

To answer the questions on this page, you will have to recall scientific facts and draw upon your knowledge of how science works, e.g. scientific procedures, issues and ideas.

1 Read the following information about biodiesel carefully, before answering the questions below.

Biodiesel Factsheet

Biodiesel is a liquid fuel, which can be used to power motor transport in place of diesel. It is produced from crops like cereals, oilseeds and sugar beet, so is wholly renewable. It emits 50–60% less carbon dioxide than a fossil fuel and is biodegradable.

However, the energy content of biodiesel is around 11% less per gallon than diesel and it costs nearly twice as much to produce.

No engine modifications are needed to use biodiesel, which can be used on its own or blended with mineral diesel. At the moment, it is most commonly used as a 5% blend, as this meets with vehicle manufacturer warranties.

Biodiesel made from recycled vegetable oil is only available from around 100 filling stations, but this could increase with demand. There are ample crop supplies and farm land in the UK to cope with growth in this market.

---

a) Summarise the advantages and disadvantages of biodiesel compared to diesel in the table below.

Advantages	Disadvantages

b) At the moment, the UK relies on foreign imports to meet its demand for transport fuels. With this in mind, describe how using more biodiesel instead of diesel would affect the economy and environment.

How Science Works

To answer the questions on this page, you will have to recall scientific facts and draw upon your knowledge of how science works, e.g. scientific procedures, issues and ideas.

1 Hydrogen gas and chlorine gas react to form hydrogen chloride gas. Here is the word and symbol equation for the reaction:

Hydrogen + Chlorine $\longrightarrow$ Hydrogen chloride

$H_2 + Cl_2 \longrightarrow 2HCl$

The bond energies in kJ/mol are:

H–H = 436 kJ/mol
Cl–Cl = 242 kJ/mol
H–Cl = 431 kJ/mol

a) Calculate the amount of energy needed to break the bonds of the reactants in this reaction.

_____

_____

b) Calculate the amount of energy needed to form the bonds in the products of this reaction.

_____

_____

c) Calculate the total energy change that takes place during this reaction.

_____

d) Is the reaction exothermic or endothermic? Explain your answer.

_____

_____

e) Draw a simple energy level diagram to represent this reaction.

Flame Tests

1 Complete the table alongside, to show the results produced by different compounds in a flame test.

Type of Compound	Flame Colour
Copper	
Potassium	
	Apple green
	Brick Red
Lithium	
	Yellow

Reaction of Carbonates with Dilute Acid

2 a) Which gas is produced when carbonates react with dilute acids?

b) In the space below, sketch the apparatus that can be used to test for the production of this gas.

Thermal Decomposition of Copper and Zinc Carbonate

3 When copper carbonate and zinc carbonate are heated, a thermal decomposition reaction takes place.

Write a symbol equation for each of these thermal decomposition reactions and colour in the combustion tubes below, to show what the products would look like.

i) copper carbonate.

Equation:

ii) zinc carbonate.

Equation:

Metal Ions

1 Metal compounds in solution contain metal ions. Some of these form precipitates when sodium hydroxide is added to them.

a) i) Write a symbol equation to show how a precipitate is formed when sodium hydroxide is added to a solution containing aluminium ions (Al^{3+}).

....

ii) Which precipitate is formed in this reaction? ....

iii) What colour is the precipitate? ....

b) i) Write a symbol equation to show how a precipitate is formed when sodium hydroxide is added to a solution containing copper ions (Cu^{2+}).

....

ii) Which precipitate is formed in this reaction? ....

iii) What colour is the precipitate? ....

c) i) Write a symbol equation to show how a precipitate is formed when sodium hydroxide is added to a solution containing iron ions (Fe^{2+}).

....

ii) Which precipitate is formed in this reaction? ....

iii) What colour is the precipitate? ....

2 a) Which gas is produced when sodium hydroxide is added to nitrate ions in solution?

....

b) Describe a simple test for the presence of this gas.

....

....

c) Write a symbol equation for this reaction.

....

Tests for Organic Compounds

1 There needs to be a plentiful supply of oxygen in order for the complete combustion of a fuel to take place.

a) What colour is the flame produced when the complete combustion of methane gas takes place?

_____

b) Write **i)** a word equation and **ii)** a symbol equation to show this reaction.

i) _____

ii) _____

c) What are the products of this reaction?

_____

2 If there is insufficient oxygen for complete combustion, incomplete combustion takes place.

a) What colour is the flame produced when incomplete combustion of methane gas takes place?

_____

b) Write **i)** a word equation and **ii)** a symbol equation to show this reaction.

i) _____

ii) _____

c) What are the products of this reaction?

_____

3 In terms of gas appliances (e.g. cookers and fires), why is incomplete combustion a serious problem?

_____

_____

4 Describe how bromine water can be used to identify an unsaturated organic compound (i.e. a compound with one or more double carbon carbon bonds).

_____

_____

_____

_____

HT ## Empirical Formula

1 **a)** What does the empirical formula of a compound show?

_____

b) In general terms, describe how the empirical formula of an organic compound can be found.

_____

_____

_____

2 44g of carbon dioxide and 27g of water are produced when 15g of an organic substance is burnt completely in oxygen.

a) What is the relative formula mass (M_r) of carbon dioxide?

_____

b) How much carbon is there in 44g of carbon dioxide?

_____

_____

c) What is the relative formula mass (M_r) of water?

_____

d) How much hydrogen is there in 27g of water?

_____

_____

e) What is the ratio of carbon to hydrogen involved in this reaction?

_____

_____

f) What is the empirical formula of the original organic compound in this reaction?

_____

Instrumental Methods

1 a) Give one example of an instrumental method which is used to identify elements.

b) Give three examples of instrumental methods used to identify compounds.

i)

ii)

iii)

2 List **a)** three advantages and **b)** three disadvantages of using new instrumental methods to identify elements and compounds, rather than more traditional laboratory techniques.

a) Advantages of instrumental methods:

i)

ii)

iii)

b) Disadvantages of instrumental methods:

i)

ii)

iii)

3 Unscramble the letters below to find six industries in which instrumental methods for analysing substances are commonly used.

a) INCFROSE INCCESE

b) VARMINTLEENON HALTHE

c) DIMENICE

d) FODO SIDRUNTY

e) ALICERUGRUT

f) VARYENTIRE NICESEC

4 Suggest two ways in which instruments have developed over recent years due to advances in technology.

Across

2. The block of metallic elements between Groups 2 and 3 of the Periodic Table. (10)
4. A measure of the average mass of all the isotopes for a particular element. (6,4)
8. A formula that shows the relative amounts of elements in a compound. (9)
9. Used to describe water that contains lots of mineral salts. (4)
11. The extent to which a substance can be dissolved in a solute; can be represented by a curve. (10)
13. A mathematical word used to describe relative amounts. (5)
14. Vertical columns of elements in the Periodic Table. (6)
15. The energy required to raise the temperature of 1g of water by 1°C. (7)

Down

1. The process of boiling a liquid and collecting its vapours by condensation. (12)
3. A method used to find the concentration of a known reactant. (9)
5. These can be found in solutions of metal compounds. (4)
6. A horizontal row of elements in the Periodic Table. (6)
7. A procedure used to find the amount of heat energy released by a substance when burnt. (11)
8. A type of structure; describes the arrangement of electrons in an atom. (10)
10. Close examination; breaking a substance down and identifying the separate parts. (8)
12. A unit of energy and work. (5)